Hyde Park

A play

Graham Swannell

Samuel French—London
New York—Toronto —Hollywood

CHARACTERS

Yvonne
Lawrence, her husband
Fraser, their friend
Gina, Lawrence's assistant

The action takes place in Yvonne's and Lawrence's garden

Time—the present

HYDE PARK

Yvonne's and Lawrence's garden. Birdsong

Yvonne opens the double doors and comes out into the garden. She is followed by Fraser. They have wine glasses and Yvonne has a half-bottle of wine

Yvonne stretches and yawns

Yvonne Mmnn... Goodness it's hot today.

Fraser Yes, it's hot all right.

Yvonne If we had a hammock, we could sleep all afternoon. (*She yawns*)

Fraser Yes, it was a wonderful Sunday lunch.

Yvonne Oh... I cook all the time.

Fraser Well, I haven't had a lunch like that for years. It's good to see someone is still keeping up the old traditions.

Yvonne Mmnn...

Fraser What is it?

Yvonne I want a kiss.

Fraser A what?

Yvonne You never gave me a kiss. When you appeared at the door, you never kissed me.

Fraser kisses Yvonne on the cheek

That wasn't much of a kiss.

Fraser It's true, I should have dropped you a card. In fact, I should have done many things, but you know how it is, don't you?

Yvonne Oh yes, I know.

Fraser Actually I was just sitting there. I was there and then I was here. (*He laughs*) You are sure you didn't mind me just turning up?

Yvonne You're our oldest friend, Fraser. It's always open house to you. Anyway it was just us today. Lawrence's new assistant might come later.

Fraser Who?

Yvonne Here, let me top you up.

Fraser Yes, thanks.

Yvonne fills both glasses

Well... to your new house.

Yvonne Yes. The house.

They drink

So what do you think of it? I'd have liked something bigger, but after years of flats, I suppose it's all right. Mind you, I could do without that over there. Have you ever seen a roof extension as big as that? I'm sure they never went to the Council. They probably haven't even got fire doors. You know what it means, don't you?

Fraser No.

Yvonne It means we've lost some of our sky. I stand at the window and all I see is their roof extension. Sometimes I see this woman over there looking at me. She's usually brushing her hair. She brushes her hair and smiles. Whether she's smiling at me or herself, I don't know, but I don't want to see her smiling. I want to see the sky.

Fraser You must plant a tree. A Silver Birch or Cherry.

Yvonne A tree?

Fraser I've always wanted to plant a tree.

Yvonne No, a tree would mean even less sky. Then there's the leaves in the autumn, and who do you think would have to cope with that? Well? Who?

Fraser Yes... well... I thought the fireplace in the living-room was exceptional.

Yvonne You think so?

Fraser Is it original?

Yvonne You like fires, do you?

Fraser Yes, in the winter.

Yvonne That was Lawrence's contribution. He found it at one of his auctions. He usually just buys for the shop, but this time he thought of us. Mind you, they're very dirty... fires. They also have to be cleaned out in the morning, and the smell clings to the curtains, and it's murder getting kindling these days. They tell me they used to do bags of the stuff at the grocer's round the corner. This old lady used to chop it, but now they've stopped.

Fraser Why's that?

Yvonne How should I know?

Fraser Perhaps she died.

Yvonne Died? No.

Fraser But why don't you do your own?

Yvonne We haven't got an axe.

Fraser Ah.

They drink

Yvonne Mmnn... so what about you?

Fraser Me? I haven't got an axe either.

Yvonne No, I mean, so you went off, did you? I wondered where you'd gone. I asked Lawrence, but he said you'd just gone. So you just took off, eh?

Fraser Yes, that's it.

Yvonne Off to Spain?

Fraser That's right.

Yvonne It must have been something special for you to leave the Academy.

Fraser No, I'm back. I'm back on the magazine. I'm on tributes, that kind of thing.

Yvonne Not articles?

Fraser I'm on tributes—small pieces. Anyway I'm back.

Yvonne So what was it like?

Fraser What was it like? Spain? Well... it was fine at first. Warm days and starlit nights. The bad weather came in July. The wind came first from the south-east, out of the Basque country. Then it turned north-west off the ocean and brought in cloud and rain. The cloud was low enough to touch and the rain cold. At night I went to sleep thinking it would blow out by the morning, but it never did, not while I was there.

Pause

Yvonne Well...   (*She laughs*)

Fraser Yes, that was it.

Yvonne Sounds desperate to me.

Fraser Desperate, does it? No, I had time.

Yvonne What for?

Fraser I walked miles every day.

Yvonne This doesn't sound like you, Fraser.

Fraser No, I liked it.

Yvonne Oh, yes? So who was she?

Fraser She?

Yvonne Who was the lucky lady who commandeered you? It wasn't that black-haired girl in the Tapas Bar? The one with the stud in her nose? She's always leaning all over you.

Fraser She's from Andalusia, Yvonne.

Yvonne So?

Fraser I was on my own.

Yvonne *On your own ?* You? (*She laughs*) Really?

Fraser I've been on my own for some time.

Yvonne You mean, there was no one to snuggle up against in the wind and rain?

Fraser No, I was on my own.

Yvonne Oh. (*Slight pause*) So what happened to the redhead?

Fraser The redhead?

Yvonne That redhead you brought to our flat. It was our summer party last year. You know, what was her name? She had red hair, long legs. You made a striking couple. I was jealous of her.

Fraser Jealous?

Yvonne It was the way she draped herself around you. She laughed. She had such fun. It quite spoilt my party.

Fraser What do you mean?

Yvonne I mean, it spoilt my party.

Pause

Fraser She even liked exhibitions, you know. I took her to private viewings and she enjoyed herself. Afterwards we'd find a quiet place—Greek usually. She liked Greek. She liked art. She could have been an artist. She had the eye. The first place I took her was the Courtauld Galleries. She couldn't get over the colours. I was there the other day. I went back, I don't know why. There's this Alfred Sisley, *Boats on the Seine*. I was looking at it. It's blue. Blue sky, blue river—and I was standing in front of it and some people came and stood next to me and then moved on... to other paintings, but some, some lingered, and it occurred to me as I stood there, I mean, I began to think, I wonder if they're seeing what I'm seeing? I mean, what are they seeing? What does it look like through their eyes? What does it mean, if in fact it means anything—and I began to get quite, well, I began to feel agitated, because it occurred to me we might not be seeing the same thing at all. You know? What am I saying? I'm saying I felt very cold. She went back to her husband. That's what happened to her. I went to Spain.

Pause

Yvonne Yes, I've worked hard on this house. My life has turned into a colour chart. Rose white, apple white. I wouldn't mind the work if only he said, that's nice or well done, once in a while. I'm the one who has done it, you see. Even the tiles in the bathroom. Here, finish the bottle.

Fraser No, you finish it.

Yvonne pours the drink

Yvonne You'd think he'd show some interest, wouldn't you? It is his home as well as mine.

Fraser What's wrong, Yvonne? You and Lawrence, you're all right, aren't you? (*Brief pause*) Yes of course you are. I mean, you've been married for years.

Yvonne Seventeen.

Fraser What?

Yvonne Seventeen years.

Fraser Is it really? Well, that is some achievement, isn't it? I don't know anyone who has lasted that long. Only Sean and Pat have lasted that long. I mean, these days, when I meet people

I know, I don't say," Hello, how are you?" I say, "Hello, still married?" (*He laughs*)

Yvonne Sean and Pat have separated.

Fraser What? Separated?

Yvonne While you were off with your Spanish señorita.

Fraser No. Really?

Yvonne It's back to the singles bar for Pat.

Fraser Good grief. (*He laughs*) You know, of all the couples, I thought they were the happiest. I envied them their life.

Yvonne Pat happy?

Fraser Wasn't she?

Yvonne She threw him out.

Fraser Threw old Sean out? Why?

Yvonne Why? (*She laughs*)

Fraser Dear God, what's the matter with everyone? I mean, we all go back so far. I remember you. You had all that hair then. All those curls all over your shoulders. It used to bounce, your hair, as you walked up Broadhurst Gardens. Sometimes you wore a scarf. Your hair was hidden by this scarf, but it was still there... bouncing. What happened to your hair?

Yvonne I got married.

Fraser No, I mean, I remember you and Patricia in Hyde Park.

Yvonne Hyde Park? What were we doing in Hyde Park?

Fraser You were both in white with carnations in your hair.

Yvonne Oh, you mean that concert?

Fraser Yes, that concert.

Yvonne I was still at school.

Fraser Yes, the Stones' concert. Brian Jones. The swimming pool. And I missed it. I came out of the tube at Marble Arch and everyone was walking away. I couldn't believe it. They were streaming towards the tubes and buses. They were laughing and smiling. How can anyone have missed it? It was free too. And there you were... with Pat... sitting in front of the stage. You were watching it being dismantled. I came up to you—but all you could talk about was Charlie Watts.

Yvonne Charlie Watts?

Fraser You were mad about drummers in those days.

Yvonne Poor old Charlie Watts. He's aged, hasn't he?

Fraser Yes, it's all coming back. You know, I can tell you now...
I mean, that day in the park, I was completely overwhelmed
with the desire to go to bed with you.

Yvonne What?

Fraser Whether it was the white dress, the carnation, or the fact
you'd seen the Stones, I don't know, but you weren't interested
in me. In fact, that's what the sixties were really like for me.
Missed concerts and girls in white dresses that I failed to get
into bed.

Yvonne You've made up for it since.

Fraser Have I?

Yvonne Wait a minute. You? You were overwhelmed with the
desire to go to bed... with *me* ?

Fraser Of course.

Yvonne *You were ?*

Fraser Yes, surely you knew?

Yvonne No, of course I didn't know.

Fraser You didn't?

Yvonne No.

Fraser Oh, I thought you knew.

Yvonne Knew? I hadn't a clue.

Fraser But I was so obvious.

Yvonne Not to me you weren't. I mean... if I'd known...

Fraser What?

Yvonne Well... you know... if I'd known...

Fraser You mean?

Yvonne Oh, yes.

Fraser No.

Yvonne Yes, of course. I always fancied you.

Fraser I don't believe it.

Yvonne But you must have known that.

Fraser No. Never.

Yvonne Then you were blind.

Fraser Yes, I must have been.

Yvonne I always wanted you. Always.

Fraser This is breaking my heart.

Yvonne Good.

Fraser (*angrily*) But how was I to know that? After Charlie Watts, all you and Pat talked about was Lawrence and Sean. You were going to meet them off the boat train!

Yvonne But I once said to you—we were lying on a bed at the time... there were heaps of bodies all over the place—I said to you, one day when we grow up, you and I will have an affair.

Fraser Affair?

Yvonne We were lying quite close to each other.

Fraser I don't remember that.

Yvonne Don't you?

Fraser When was that?

Yvonne Oh... sometime in the past.

Gina and Lawrence enter, laughing. Lawrence has a glass of wine and a bottle of wine

Lawrence Caught you! What are you doing with my wife?

Yvonne He's making a pass.

Lawrence Ah, well, that's all right. I thought for a moment you were talking about me.

Yvonne You, Lawrence? Why would we talk about you?

Fraser We were actually talking about Hyde Park.

Lawrence Hyde Park? What's happening in Hyde Park? You're not going on a march, are you? I went on a march once. It was... oh, years ago. Nothing happened of course. We all shouted our heads off, but nothing changed. This is Gina, by the way. My new assistant. She's brilliant with French polish. Say hello,

Gina.

Gina Hello.

Fraser Hello. My name's Fraser.

Gina Yes, I know who you are. He's always talking about you.

Lawrence Talking about *him* ? You must be joking.

Gina He's always going on about your good old days together...
when you were young and free. (*She laughs*) He gets very
nostalgic after lunch.

Yvonne Of course the young are never nostalgic. That's because
they don't have a past. They only have a future. Isn't that true,
Gina?

Pause

Lawrence Yes... well.. the funny thing about Fraser is he's still
free. (*He laughs*) That's the funny thing. He's one of life's
lucky ones. He has such a good time all the time, he hasn't got
time to drop us a line.

Fraser I know, I forgot.

Lawrence Of course you forgot. It was all those Flamenco
dancers. One on each arm, wasn't it? God, I envy you.

Yvonne Do you, Lawrence?

Lawrence Of course I do. I mean, of course I don't. Oh, you
know what I mean.

Yvonne Yes, I know. (*Slight pause*) Actually Lawrence once
went on a Fun Run in Hyde Park.

Fraser A Fun Run?

Lawrence Watch it, Fraser.

Fraser Were you drunk?

Lawrence I was raising money for some charity. I was doing my
bit. It was hell, but I did it.

Yvonne It's true. I had to wait for him by Spekes Monument.
When he returned he was a hideous colour.

Lawrence I was too! (*He laughs*)

Gina Oh no, I can't believe that. Lawrence is an excellent runner.

Lawrence I wasn't then, G.

Yvonne Gina runs too, don't you, Gina?

Gina Oh yes, every morning. Wet or dry. It's great fun.

Yvonne What? What did she say? (*She laughs*) Fun? It's not my idea of fun. It's not yours either, is it, Lawrence?

Pause

Lawrence More wine, Fraser?

Fraser Yes, thanks.

Lawrence pours a drink

Actually we were remembering the Stones' concert in Hyde Park.

Lawrence Oh, that. I don't think I saw that one.

Yvonne You were on a train.

Lawrence Was I? What was I doing on a train? I haven't been on a train for years.

Gina I thought you told me you saw the Stones' concert.

Lawrence What's that?

Gina You said you were there.

Lawrence Oh, no, that was Blind Faith.

Gina No, it wasn't. Blind Faith? Who's Blind Faith?

Lawrence (*mocking*) Who's Blind Faith?

Gina But he told me he saw them, Fraser. He said he was with you.

Fraser Me? No, I missed it too. Got the wrong time. Story of my life.

Yvonne Well, I saw it. I was there. I'll never forget it. Jagger reading Shelley. It was such a ... well, it was one of those days. Sometimes I think it must be terrible to be your age, Gina. You were one in sixty-nine, weren't you? I mean, you were hardly alive.

Gina That's true. Mind you, I've made up for it since.

Yvonne Yes... I'm sure you have. Has Lawrence told you about his new love, Fraser?

Lawrence My new love?

Yvonne It's ... golf.

Fraser Golf?

Lawrence Yes, it's a great game, Fraser. You should try it.

Yvonne He's ruined the lawn. I mean, look at it. There's divots everywhere.

Lawrence All right, Yvonne.

Yvonne He comes out here all hours to practise his swing. I've even known him get up at six, practice his swing and then go off for a jog. I belong to a group, "Women against Golf". As you can imagine, we're not very popular with the chaps.

Gina I don't know what you mean, Yvonne. Lawrence's swing is very fluid.

Yvonne Is it really.

Gina Well, the club professional thinks so.

Yvonne What? You've been to the club?

Gina Yes, didn't Lawrence tell you?

Yvonne No.

Gina Oh... he's been giving me lessons.

Yvonne Oh... has he?

Gina Yes, he's awfully helpful.

Yvonne Awfully helpful—really?

Lawrence All right, Yvonne.

Gina It's my slice, you see. I slice to the right.

Lawrence It's her hips actually. She has trouble swivelling them.

Yvonne Now that is a surprise.

Gina No, it's not my hips, it's my——

Lawrence (*abruptly*) All right, Gina.

Gina What? Have I said something wrong?

Yvonne My God, I don't know, do you, Fraser? Here I am killing myself getting this house off the ground, and all he does is give her golf lessons. That is when he's not out buying mallet-shaped decanters with mushroom stoppers. I mean, we've got a shop full of decanters.

Lawrence I like decanters.

Yvonne Your problem is you can't bear to sell them, can you? You buy all these useless articles, and then hoard the lot. You won't even sell those football cigarette cards.

Lawrence Oh no, they're inviolate. They're pre-war, Fraser.

Yvonne (*bitterly*) If you sold them we might be able to afford a holiday. I can't remember the last time we had a holiday!

Lawrence Yes. Well. (*He laughs*) I'm going to open another bottle.

Yvonne Yes, you do that.

Lawrence I think it's time for the old Bordeaux. Are you coming, Gina?

Gina What?

Yvonne He wants you to help him with the corkscrew.

Gina Did I say something wrong?

Lawrence Come on, Gina!

Lawrence and Gina exit. Lawrence slams the door

Pause. Birdsong

Fraser Are you all right, Yvonne?

Yvonne Of course I'm all right! (*Brief pause*) I'm sorry, I didn't mean to snap. I'm just jealous, that's all. It's perfectly straightforward.

Fraser Oh no, I'm sure there's nothing going on, Yvonne.

Yvonne You think I care?

Fraser Of course you care.

Yvonne That is where you are wrong. You don't really know me, do you? We may go back years, but we're still strangers. I'm only jealous of Lawrence because he has all the fun.

Fraser Fun? What fun?

Yvonne The fun you've been having all your life. God, I envy you.

Fraser My life's not fun. (*He laughs*)

Yvonne You should try living mine for a while. You think we don't know when we take you in our arms? We may pretend we don't know, but we know.

Fraser Know what?

Yvonne Oh, I really do like you, Fraser. Come on, give me a kiss. (*Brief pause*) No? Well, at least sit with me on the bench. Sit with me... please...

They sit. Pause

What a heavenly day. It's the kind of day that cries out for an assignation.

Fraser A *what* ?

Yvonne Sometimes I long to wake up somewhere else. I don't know where—Vienna perhaps. I'd like to sit in a café all morning—perhaps a meeting later—behind closed shutters. That's my idea of fun.

Fraser No. You'd soon tire of it.

Yvonne You think so?

Fraser Yes, I've done all that. You know, that kind of thing— all those snatched hours. It's all right while it's going on, but afterwards... She went back to her husband, you know. (*Brief pause*) I always thought you were both...

Yvonne All right?

Fraser You know... while I was in Spain, I spent most of my time walking the beach. At first, in the good weather, the beaches were packed. There were all these men and women looking at each other. Checking each other out. You could virtually hear them thinking, would it be any better with him? What about her? She looks more my type. All that flesh, all that sun tan oil, all that... fun. And yet, strangely, over it all, there was this overpowering sense of desperation, of... ennui.

Yvonne What are you telling me?

Fraser I'm telling you, at the end of the day, when they'd all gone back to their hotels, all that was left was this... detritus. The beach was covered in plastic bottles, cans, cigarette ends. The tide cleared some of it, but it only brought it back the next day. (*Brief pause*) Yes, you'd soon tire of it. I know I finally have. It was only when the bad weather came, and the beach emptied, that I at last felt... comfortable.

Pause

Yvonne I'd like to tell you something about me.

Fraser No, please. It's your private life. It's not for me to know.

Yvonne Old age... terrifies me.

Fraser What?

Yvonne I'm getting older by the month. Where's the happiness in that process?

Fraser Oh, come off it, Yvonne. You're not old.

Yvonne And you're a man. What do you know about it? Old age is a woman's greatest punishment.

Fraser But Yvonne, you're not even forty.

Yvonne I look into your face and see how I've aged. (*Brief pause*) I mean, look at my knees.

Fraser Your knees?

Yvonne They're starting to sag.

Fraser Sag?

Yvonne Yes, look. Look at my poor knees.

Fraser No, no, you've always had terrific knees.

Yvonne Not any more.

Fraser No, it's true. Terrific knees. Terrific legs in fact. Terrific you know.

Yvonne Yes... (*Brief pause*) Really?

Fraser I should say so.

Yvonne In that case I ought to flaunt them more before they do
sag. Because they will, eventually. It will all sag, eventually.
We're not born sinful, Fraser. It's old age that's the great sin.
(*Brief pause*) I've never mentioned it before, but you've got
tremendous teeth.

Fraser I brush them twice a day.

Yvonne It's not wrong to want a little fun, is it? I've had my fill
of doing up this place. I'm sick to death of picking up items I
didn't drop. I mean, why should I do it? Sometimes, when I go
out, I'm so out of sorts, I think I'm going to fall off the planet.
That kind of thing makes you want to hold something—a pair
of shoulders for instance...I think it's time you gave me a decent
kiss.

They kiss

Mmnn. (*She laughs*) Why are you looking at me like that?

Fraser I'm the one who should have married you.

Yvonne Oh yes?

Fraser If I was your husband, I wouldn't be in there with that
child.

Yvonne Wouldn't you? Where would you be?

Fraser Out here with you.

Pause

Yvonne I think we should meet up in town. We could have a
coffee in the *Torino* after you've finished at the Academy. We
could sit and have coffee and talk and then go for a walk in the
park. We could walk across Hyde Park to Paddington.

Fraser I live in Paddington.

Yvonne I know.

Fraser What do you mean?

Yvonne You have a view of the park, don't you? I mean, do you wake up and have your coffee looking at the park? Do you stand there in your dressing-gown or are you naked?

Fraser I don't have a dressing-gown.

Yvonne No, I mean, do people stop over in your flat? Do you have people with you or are you always alone when you wake? I'm never alone. I wake up and the first thing I see is the back of Lawrence's head. His hair sticks up in the morning. He's slumped there with his hair sticking up. Of course, he has less hair now than he used to have, but what hair he has still manages to stick up. And there you are with your view of the park. You don't know how lucky you are. I think I better come to your flat tomorrow.

Fraser Tomorrow?

Yvonne In the morning.

Fraser I'm out in the morning.

Yvonne I'll come in the afternoon.

Fraser I'm also out in the afternoon.

Yvonne Then I'll come on Tuesday. I'll bring a hamper. What would you like? Some cheese? A selection of cheeses. And some paté. I'm very big on mackerel paté at the moment. And afterwards, some cold meat, a tossed salad...

Fraser You're thinking of more than one meal?

Yvonne Mmnn... I'm famished.

Fraser What?

Yvonne I'm suffering from extreme hunger.

Fraser But we've just had lunch.

Yvonne You know what I mean.

Fraser No, the point is, Yvonne, I used to wake up shattered.

Yvonne What? Shattered?

Fraser I'd get back at night shattered, and then wake shattered. Some years back I could still take it. I mean, I used to be

hopping about all over the place some years back... getting by
on three or four hours a night... and then jumping out of bed first
thing, and you know, generally putting myself about with a
certain amount of relish. Now I'm just shattered by all that.
That's why I liked Spain. I had time to put my feet up—I mean,
when I wasn't out walking. I could put my feet up or go out for
a walk, you know, on my own, and then I'd come back and I
found for some reason, I always woke quite refreshed the next
day. I used to open my eyes and I wasn't shattered. I'd get up
and have a cup of tea and look out of the window. I used to
watch the rain. Then I'd get back into bed and read, or not
read—just lie there sometimes... breathing. I've tried to con-
tinue like that since I've been back. Once or twice I've woken
up shattered, but they were mistakes. Have you ever tried lying
there just breathing?

Yvonne You mean I'm too old?

Fraser What?

Yvonne You prefer your women young. You prefer the new
bloom like Lawrence.

Fraser No, I don't think you understood me.

Yvonne I remember that day you came up in the park. The sun
was behind you. You looked so... but all you could talk about
was how you'd missed the concert... you kept going on about
it...

Fraser No, stop this, Yvonne. I think Lawrence is watching us.

Yvonne Haven't you ever felt that you'd just like it, and forget
everything else? You'd like to throw everything off and forget
all the stuff. The everyday stuff. Just get back to what it was like
when it was then, and you were there, and you were in your
body. You could feel your body and it felt right. The skin was
right and you just fell into it. You just fell and kept on falling
until you nearly disappeared in all that skin, and you ached, you
ached all day, until you fell once more, and once was never
enough, was it?

Fraser (*after a pause*) I think I better go.

Yvonne *Go?*

Fraser Yes, I must go. I've some unfinished work.

Yvonne No.

Fraser I must finish my piece. It's an obituary in fact. One of those people no-one ever knew. Who regularly sent their three paintings to the Academy each summer.

Yvonne Don't talk to me about paintings. You used to come and sit by our paraffin stove in Broadhurst Gardens. You used to sit and smoke and talk about paintings by Mark Rothko. We'd fall asleep and when we woke you'd still be talking about this Mark Rothko. In fact, you were going to be Mark Rothko.

Fraser He killed himself.

Yvonne You never became anyone. (*Slight pause*) I mean, what's happened to you? You used to be a good laugh. You've changed. I'm like the people on your beach. I love all that. I love holidays and checking my tan at the end of the day. I don't want to put my feet up. I don't want to lie somewhere just breathing. I made a mistake. I thought you were someone else. Yes, I mistook you for someone who once had fun.

Fraser But I love you.

Yvonne What?

Fraser I've always loved you.

Yvonne What does that mean?

Fraser It means I'm off. Because if we meet up, I would only love you more.

Yvonne (*laughing*) Love me more?

Fraser Yes... but you would go home afterwards.

Yvonne You love me?

Fraser Absolutely.

Yvonne (*shocked*) My God. (*Brief pause*) Really?

Fraser You are so...

Yvonne What? What?

Fraser Yes, all right, tomorrow. I've always been a fool. It's what I want. You. Tomorrow.

Yvonne Tomorrow?

Fraser Yes, tomorrow.

Yvonne You're out tomorrow.

Fraser No, I'm in tomorrow. I can be in all day.

Yvonne Yes... well... you're in, are you?

Fraser I'll be there.

Yvonne Oh, right.

Fraser I'll be at the window. What time?

Yvonne Time?

Fraser Morning or afternoon?

Yvonne Tomorrow?

Fraser I was such a fool. I took the wrong route. I knew you were my route, but I never took it. We would have been right together. We will be right together! (*He laughs*) It should have been me always. But I thought that was all for the past. All that marriage stuff. A thing of the past. I knew a better route. What a fool. No-one told me you ended up in a room talking to yourself. I knew I had to come here today. I was in my chair, then I was here. I knew I had to do it.

Yvonne You came for me?

Fraser I don't know why I came.

Yvonne No, stop it, Fraser. He's watching us.

Fraser You're so right for me. You've no idea how much I'll love you.

Yvonne (*abruptly*) Yes. Well. Look. Actually, you know, I wasn't...

Fraser What?

Yvonne I wasn't... look, I've got this plasterer coming tomorrow.

Fraser What?

Yvonne We've a crack in our extension. We've some damp. It needs new plaster. Well, that's what they tell me. Of course, they're all liars, but that's what they say.

Fraser So? Tuesday then?

Yvonne No, it's all week actually. I have to be here. You know, tea, coffee, more tea, biscuits. I have to keep an eye. I ought to be here.

Pause

Fraser You have to be here?

Yvonne I ought to.

Fraser What are you saying?

Yvonne I should be here.

Fraser What are you talking about?

Yvonne Well, I was talking about fun, not love.

Fraser What are you talking about?

Lawrence enters with a decanter full of wine and a glass. There is a burst of music as he opens the doors, The Beach Boys "I Get Around." The music fades as he shuts the doors

Lawrence Hey you! The one with the sagging knees.

Yvonne My knees don't sag.

Lawrence That's not what she told me, Fraser. (*He laughs*) Listen, listen, it's not a crime to like golf. Golf is the ultimate game. It's you against yourself. It humbles you. Until you've taken ten at the first hole, you'll never know how useless you are. Here, have another drink, Fraser.

Fraser No thanks, Lawrence. I'm off.

Lawrence Off? *Off* ?

Fraser I've work to do. I've an article to complete.

Lawrence Oh no, no, you're not off. We're going to make a night of it. I mean, I've gone and dug the old Beach Boys out. (*Singing*) "We've been having fun all summer long." (*He laughs*) You remember that day? That day when we were hitching out to Clacton? And that guy switched on his radio and

the Beach Boys were playing. It was the day I came alive. You
should have seen us, Yvonne. We were only thirteen and we
pretended we were crashing out of the Mojave desert and
bowling down to L.A. to catch the surf. I've always wanted to
catch the surf. Here, come and drink with me. I can't stand
drinking alone.

Fraser No, Lawrence, I really must go.

Lawrence But I haven't had a session with you for ages. I mean,
hell, we hardly ever talk any more.

Yvonne Oh, let him go, Lawrence.

Lawrence Why? Why should I? I'm up to here doing what you
tell me to do. I was perfectly happy in that flat.

Yvonne What?

Lawrence Oh, Fraser, Fraser... I've just opened my best claret.
I've decanted it for you. It's been having a breathe. Isn't this a
beautiful decanter? I got it out near Southwold. It was a bitch
of a day. Gales. Rain. You know, the full house. Still it was
worth it... to have this... look at the light through it.

Fraser Lawrence.

Lawrence What?

Fraser A word of advice.

Lawrence Oh yes?

Fraser Stop hacking round golf courses.

Lawrence What?

Fraser You were always lucky. I'd hate to see you run out of
luck.

Lawrence Me? Lucky? What's he talking about, Yvonne?

Yvonne How should I know.

Fraser My father once said to me, "You have fresh orange juice,
cod liver oil capsules, three meals a day, you live in a centrally
heated house, and all you can think about is sex." "No, love."
I replied. I was so pompous. He said I was ridiculous to believe
in the existence of love. I said he was ridiculous to have married
my mother if he didn't love her.

Lawrence What did he say to that?

Fraser He didn't say anything. He just gave me a right hook which knocked me out.

Lawrence Quite right too, I always liked your father.

Fraser Look to your wife, Lawrence.

Lawrence What? My wife? Does he mean you, Yvonne?

Yvonne Ask him.

Lawrence Look to her? What's that supposed to mean? What's going on, Fraser? Do you know something that I don't know? I mean, what am I supposed to know that I don't already know? Eh? Yvonne? Christ! I've just opened my best bottle. I've been saving it for such a day. Fraser? What did you mean?

Fraser Goodbye, Lawrence.

Lawrence Hey, Fraser, you can't go. What about one for old times. One for old Hyde Park.

Fraser Hyde Park? Hyde Park never happened. They just made money, that's all.

Lawrence What?

Fraser Take care, Yvonne.

Lawrence Fraser!

Fraser exits

There is a burst of music as he opens the doors, The Beach Boys, "California Girls". The music fades as he shuts the doors. Pause

Yvonne Well... he's gone.

Lawrence pours a drink and drinks

Lawrence (*laughing*) What was all that about?

Yvonne God knows.

Lawrence Well, you were talking to him. Was it something you said?

Yvonne No.

Lawrence So what were you talking about?

Yvonne Oh... nothing.

Lawrence Well, something's got into him. Are you sure you weren't having a good bitch about me?

Yvonne Oh, all right... if you must know... he made a pass at me.

Lawrence So you said.

Yvonne No. He actually made... a pass.

Lawrence You're joking.

Yvonne No. It's no joke.

Lawrence You mean, he made a dart at you?

Yvonne Yes. Your friend. He made... a dart.

Lawrence My God.

Yvonne I refused of course.

Lawrence Of course.

Yvonne That's what got into him.

Lawrence Oh, I see... but that's appalling.

Yvonne I know.

Lawrence I'm appalled. I mean, who does he think we are? Turning up here. Uninvited. Eating our food. Virtually hogging the apple sauce. Drinking my drink. And then making a play for my wife. Who the hell does he think we are?

Yvonne We're his friends.

Lawrence Friends? That's ripe. What's happening here? I mean, who can you trust, if you can't trust your friends? He must be ill. He's sick. He ought to see someone. He ought to see Jack. Jack will sort him out. Poor old Fraser. Who would have thought it. Of course you know his trouble, don't you?

Yvonne No, what?

Lawrence He still thinks it's the sixties. He doesn't understand we've all grown up since that time. He still thinks The Doors are singing Hello, I Love You, Won't You Tell Me Your Name? That's his trouble.

Yvonne I never liked that record.

Lawrence Didn't you? Oh, I did. (*Slight pause*) Made a pass, did
   he?

He laughs. Yvonne walks off

   Where are you going, Yvonne?
Yvonne I'm going to bed.
Lawrence What?
Yvonne He's ruined my Sunday.
Lawrence Oh no, don't say that.
Yvonne It's completely spoilt. I'm off to bed.
Lawrence Oh, come on, it's not that bad. This kind of thing
   happens all the time.
Yvonne Not to me it doesn't.
Lawrence Yes... well...
Yvonne The truth is you don't really care he's made a pass.
Lawrence Of course I care. I'm appalled.
Yvonne No, you're not. You're not even jealous. You'd have
   done something if you were jealous.
Lawrence Done what? What is this, Yvonne? I've done nothing.
   So don't get at me.
Yvonne Nothing! Is that what you call it? This is all your fault.
Lawrence My fault?
Yvonne Yes, you're to blame.
Lawrence He made a pass, and I'm to blame?
Yvonne I'm going to bed.
Lawrence Yvonne ... don't...
Yvonne You say goodbye to Gina for me. I'm sure you'll like
   that. You're quite capable of saying that. You're quite able to
   go up to her and say that, aren't you? I mean, I could be lying
   in the gutter and you'd still be able to go up to her. You'd still
   be leaning all over her. Good-night.
Lawrence Good-night? It's only three o'clock.

Yvonne You used to be fun.
Lawrence What? Yvonne...

Yvonne exits

She leaves the doors open. The Beach Boys, "I Can Hear Music" is playing

After a while Gina enters. She closes the doors and the music fades. Pause

Gina Lawrence? (*Slight pause*) Are you all right?
Lawrence What?
Gina Where's Fraser? (*Slight pause*) Has Fraser gone?
Lawrence Yes, he's gone.
Gina Gone?
Lawrence He's gone off.
Gina Oh. (*Slight pause*) Where's Yvonne gone?
Lawrence To bed.
Gina Bed?
Lawrence She's tired. It's just us left.
Gina She's gone to bed? Is anything wrong?
Lawrence She's got a headache.
Gina It's not me, is it? I hope she didn't think...
Lawrence No, it's nothing to do with you.
Gina That's right. I've done nothing. (*Slight pause*) Are you coming back in then? I mean, have you got any other music? Isn't there anything else to play?
Lawrence What?
Gina Have you got any new music?
Lawrence What?
Gina New music, you know.
Lawrence New music?
Gina Yes, have you anything new?

Lawrence No.

Gina Oh. What, no rap?

Lawrence Rap?

Gina You know, rap?

Lawrence *Rap* ?

Gina You've got nothing new then. (*Slight pause*) Well... I think I ought to... you know... I think I might as well... Look at the time.

Lawrence What's got into everyone? It's Sunday. My day off. What's the trouble? I haven't done anything, have I? I mean, what have I done? It's nothing to do with me. I haven't touched you. I haven't laid a finger. I haven't touched anyone. Not for years. Years. What's she going on about? If that's what she thinks, perhaps I ought to. Then she really would have something to worry about, wouldn't she? Gina? Where are you going?

Gina I've got to go. I'm meeting someone. Thanks for the drink.

Lawrence Meeting someone?

Gina I've got to go. Bye.

Lawrence Oh... bye.

Gina exits. She leaves the doors ajar. Music plays, the Beach Boys,"Don't Worry, Baby"

I remember this song.

The song plays to a finish. Birdsong. Fade

FURNITURE AND PROPERTY LIST

On stage: Double doors opening to garden
                Bench

Off stage: Wine glasses (**Yvonne** and **Fraser**)
                Half-bottle of wine (**Yvonne**)
                Glass and bottle of wine (**Lawrence**)
                Decanter of wine and glass (**Lawrence**)

LIGHTING PLOT

Property fittings required: nil
Exterior. The same throughout

To open: Bright sunshine

No cues

EFFECTS PLOT

Cue 1 To open   (Page 1)
Birdsong. Fade when ready

Cue 2 **Lawrence** slams the door   (Page 13)
Birdsong. Fade when ready

Cue 3 As **Lawrence** opens the doors   (Page21)
Burst of "I Get Around" which fades as
he shuts the door

Cue 4 **Fraser** exits   (Page 23)
Burst of The Beach Boys"California Girls"
which fades as he shuts the door

Cue 5 **Yvonne** leaves the doors open   (Page 26)
Burst of The Beach Boys"I Can Hear
Music"

Cue 6 **Gina** closes the doors   (Page 26)
Music fades

Cue 7 **Gina** leaves the doors ajar   (Page 27)
The Beach Boys "Don' t Worry,Baby" plays
to a finish. Birdsong. Fade when ready

Printed by
THE KINGFISHER PRESS, LONDON NW10 6UG